YOUR KNOWLEDGE HAS VALUE

- We will publish your bachelor's and master's thesis, essays and papers

- Your own eBook and book - sold worldwide in all relevant shops

- Earn money with each sale

Upload your text at www.GRIN.com
and publish for free

Bibliographic information published by the German National Library:

The German National Library lists this publication in the National Bibliography; detailed bibliographic data are available on the Internet at http://dnb.dnb.de .

This book is copyright material and must not be copied, reproduced, transferred, distributed, leased, licensed or publicly performed or used in any way except as specifically permitted in writing by the publishers, as allowed under the terms and conditions under which it was purchased or as strictly permitted by applicable copyright law. Any unauthorized distribution or use of this text may be a direct infringement of the author s and publisher s rights and those responsible may be liable in law accordingly.

Imprint:

Copyright © 2016 GRIN Verlag
Print and binding: Books on Demand GmbH, Norderstedt Germany
ISBN: 9783668643345

This book at GRIN:

https://www.grin.com/document/413169

Sandra Samaan

The role of the Homeland Security Department in fighting domestic terrorism. The Boston Marathon bombing

GRIN - Your knowledge has value

Since its foundation in 1998, GRIN has specialized in publishing academic texts by students, college teachers and other academics as e-book and printed book. The website www.grin.com is an ideal platform for presenting term papers, final papers, scientific essays, dissertations and specialist books.

Visit us on the internet:

http://www.grin.com/

http://www.facebook.com/grincom

http://www.twitter.com/grin_com

Homeland Security; Domestic Terrorism

.(Boston Marathon Bombing Case Study)

This paper is going to focus on the role of the Homeland Security Department in defending the U.S. from a special type of terrorism, which is domestic and home-grown terrorism. Since 9/11 and all the attention has been given to protecting the country from international terrorist groups like Al-Qaeda, yet domestic terror has been repeatedly revealing itself as a serious threat facing the security of the United States. In this paper, we will discuss the challenges facing the American Homeland Security and the strategic plans to face these challenges and to prevent future human disasters from taking place. For further explanation this paper will use the Boston Marathon Bombing event as a case study for the discussed literature.

The first study used in this paper is a report by the Heritage Foundation written by Zuckerman, Jessica; Bucci, Steven P; and Carafano, James Jay about the major terrorist attacks that took place in the US after 9/11. Most of the attacks target whether the US military facilities, individual targets or mass gatherings as in our case of the Boston Marathon and others like shopping malls or nightclubs. The main concern regarding these attacks is that the actors were whether American citizens, legal permanent residents, or visitors radicalized predominantly in the United States. According to the article, out of 60 terror events that took place after 9/11, 49 were "domestic grown plots", and 77 out of the 156 people arrested or killed for plotting terrorist attacks since 9/11 are American citizens (Zuckerman, Bucci and Carafano). The Homeland Security Committee has been working very hard since 9/11 to protect the US from similar attacks, and it has been very successful with yet few failures. Out of the dozens of terror plots against the United States since September 11, 2001, 56 were foiled, mainly by the enforcement of the US law, while only four were successful. However, different measures still need to be considered in strengthening the domestic counterterrorism enterprise to insure a safer and more peaceful future for the American citizens.

The authors of this report have mentioned some of the measures that should be implemented for a safer American community such as applying a proactive rather than the current reactive policy approach. The proactive approach would work on enhancing intelligence tools instead of prosecuting terrorists. Consequently critical counterterrorism tools are required in the war on domestic terrorism. These tools include investigative ones such as the "PATRIOT Act", which includes some key provisions such as the regular supervision authority and business records provision, which through previous experience, have proved essential for thwarting terror plots. These provisions require frequent reauthorization which hinders the Homeland Security from using them when they needed to. Therefore, permanent authorization of the provisions of the PATRIOT Act is required from the Congress in order to ensure that the law enforcement and intelligence authorities have the essential counterterrorism tools they need in their war against domestic and home-grown terrorists (Zuckerman, BuccI, & Carafano).

The second article used in this paper is "Was Boston Marathon bombing a US 'intelligence failure" by Peter Grier. adding to the previous report, this article also discusses the intelligence tools used by the FBI in combating terrorism in addition to some vital components of U.S. national security are also mentioned. These components include the legitimate government surveillance programs, which succeeded to prevent over 50 incidents of terrorism both home and abroad. The author also emphasizes the importance of cooperation and information sharing among the different government levels; federal, state and local. Since the state and local law enforcement agencies represent the front line of the national security strategy, they require enough information from the federal government in general and the FBI in specific.

Local governments are prepared to identify and prevent any potential danger from "lone wolf actors" and other home born extremists while the Federal law enforcement, on the other hand, is built to battle larger cells, groups, and organizations, rather than individuals (Grier). In addition to that, financial stability and wise reallocation of resources is important in all fields and departments. Therefore, the Department of Homeland Security has to use available capabilities in a way that maximizes their benefit. To explain further, instead of adding new components to the system, officials of the law enforcement agencies and Homeland Security should streamline the domestic counterterrorism enterprise through leveraging resources and authorities among state and local governments. For example, the Department of Homeland Security can decrease the number of fusion centers, which exist in low-risk areas or areas where similar capabilities exist. This can take place by limiting funding to the fusion centers that are found outside the 31 highest risk urban areas (Grier).

The third paper used in this literature is "More training, Communication Funds Needed, First Responders Say" by Christina Munnell and Chelsea Todaro. In this paper, Munnell and Todaro recommend setting a strategy that aims at countering violent extremism. For further explanation, in August 2011, the U.S. government released a strategic plan called "Empowering local Partners to Prevent Violent Extremism in the united States." this plan set the agenda for federal agencies to assist local officials, groups, and private organizations in preventing violent extremism. Moreover, this agenda included strengthening cooperation and information sharing among law enforcement agencies as well as helping communities understand how to counter extremist propaganda especially the online-based ones (Munnell and Todaro). Furthermore, according to Munnell and Todaro, there have been other deficiencies in the emergency response of the Homeland Security Department that revealed itself during the Boston Marathon Bombing which is the insufficient training on many levels. For instance, firefighters weren't able to communicate properly while trying to save the victims. More, drills and exercises could have been used in a more efficient way to maintain preparedness and ensure a faster response.

On the other hand, Arthur L. Kellemann, Kobi Peleg and N Engl J Med explain in their article "Lessons from Boston" the positive role played by all agencies including the bystanders in limiting losses resulting from the Boston bombing terror event. Emergency Medical Services (EMS) personnel as well as law enforcement agents in minutes were in the scene with ambulances transferring the injured victims to hospitals where surgeons worked hard to save them. without the preparedness and hard work of everyone in his/her place beginning with the firefighters, the EMS, police officers, ambulance drivers and surgeons as well as bystanders who rushed to save the victims, the disaster could have been much worse and mortality rate would have been so much higher.

In this paper, the Boston Marathon Bombing is used as a case study to explain the role of Homeland Security in maintaining maximum security possible by using some of the tools mentioned above. The case study also highlights the deficiencies in HLS committee and how to overcome these deficiencies by updating the intelligence tools used as well as setting strategies for information sharing and better communication among different law enforcement agencies and government of all levels.

This terror event took place on April 15, 2013 around 2:50 pm at 671–673 and 755 Boylston Street, Boston, Massachusetts where two pressure cooker bombs exploded during a marathon event leading to the death of 3 and injured 264 others including sixteen who lost their limbs (Kellermann and Peleg). Three days later, the FBI announced that they have identified the criminals who were two Kyrgyz-American brothers named Dzhokhar Tsarnaev and Tamerlan

Tsarnaev. The two brothers have been involved in previous violent terrorism attacks on policemen and civilians. For example, they were accused of shooting an MIT policeman, kidnapping a man from his own car, and shooting out with the police in at Watertown, where they severely injured two police officers. Although raised in Europe, the two brothers believed in the ideology of extremist Islam and followed Al-Qaeda online. They claimed that they learned how to create a bomb from fireworks at home through a video that was shared online by one of Al-Qaeda members. This explains the need for more attention and supervision of the spreading ideologies within the physical borders of the country and clarifies the amount of danger of technological advancement being in the wrong hands.

There are many successes, yet there are some failures too that reveal themselves clearly in the response of the Homeland Security Department before, during and after this terror attack. According to Peleg and Shenhar, there is significant evidence that there have been national awareness and disaster preparedness not just among officials, but also within the civilian community and the health providers. As a result of previous attacks, people became aware of how to react to sudden events. in our case, there are two significant civilians who played an important role in identifying the criminals; first is the driver of the carjacked vehicle who managed to escape his captors and was smart enough to leave his cell phone intentionally in the vehicle, so that it could be traced, and second is David Henneberry who stepped into the suspect's backyard during the curfew, spotted blood on his boat, and called the police. Kellermann and Peleg explain further how the medical staff in hospitals, whom have never dealt with bombing victims, yet they have learned lessons about emergency response from military surgeons and emergency physicians. Response to Boston bombing signifies the importance of implementing a "broad-based approach to disaster preparedness" that includes federal efforts for a more flexible and all-hazards approach rather than a narrow focused one on bioterrorists and mass-destructive weapons. This issue has been one of the problems with the HLS strategy since 9/11 because it shifted the attention completely to terrorist organizations and mass destructions neglecting the danger of the equally violent home-grown terrorism. Moreover, based on Grier's article "Was boston marathon bombing a US 'intelligence failure'?" another reason for the failures of Homeland Security in the Boston Bombing case is the dysfunctionality of FBI in using technology and database systems efficiently. In our case, the criminals have been involved in previous attacks on police and civilians in different occasions, yet they were still freely moving in the country and even traveling from to other countries without appearing on FBI records simply by misspelling their names. This is a serious problem that cost the country the lives of innocent civilians racing on a state holiday peacefully. Therefore, immediate strategy should be implemented to improve the use of technology and database system within the Department of Homeland Security, the FBI as well as the state and local governments.

It is very significant that state and local governments are taking preparedness measures especially after Boston bombings since the two bombs used in the attack were homemade. according to the Mark Guarino in his article "Fourth of July events: how cities are beefing up security post Boston Marathon", measures have been taken to provide the misuse of fireworks as stated by the author "Federal Bureau of Investigation and Department of Homeland Security jointly released an alert to state and local law enforcement across the country, warning that "consumer fireworks ... can be misused by criminals and violent extremists to construct improvised explosive devices." (Guarino).

The last article used in this paper is " Policing terror threats and false positives: Employing a signal detection model to examine changes in national and local policing strategy between 2001 and 2007" by the authors John C. Kilburn Jr., Stephen E. Costanza, Eric Metchik and Kevin Borgeson. in this article, the authors provide theory based on last decade's incidents for Homeland Security decision-making policy. They name it "hypervigilance" and they defined it as "a state in which agency policy is rationally structured to maximize the pursuit of false positives and gravitate aggressively toward security threats." (Kilburn, Costanza, Metchik, and Borgeson). the main output of this study is that there is a need for quality policing and security measures rather than quantity with focus on what "signal detection model" as a suitable starting methodology for the study of such policing strategies. What the authors mean by signal detection model is that the Homeland Security Department and the FBI should use measures that help them differentiate between the important information and how to communicate it properly without getting confused by random and distracting information that could be misleading. If implemented properly, the signal detection model would play a vital role in preventing future homegrown as well as international terror disasters (Kilburn, Costanza, Metchik, and Borgeson).

Based on the previous literature and the case study on Boston Marathon Bombing, it is clear that the Department of Homeland Security developing rapidly. As mentioned above, full attention was given to terrorism from outside the country, which is mainly established terror groups such as Al Qaeda and Taliban. Yet, after the repetitive attacks that took place inland by the hands of homegrown, American terrorists, or legal visitors who found their way through the FBI detection without being noticed. There are still many measures that need to be implemented such as the urgent need for advanced database systems and better use of technology for better information sharing and detection of online terror groups. Moreover, risk preparedness is essential not only in combating terrorism, but also in rescuing victims immediately through firefighters, medical care and even normal citizens who happen to attend any terror event. As happened in Boston bombing case, people's awareness allowed them to take immediate measures which lessened the size of the disaster.

In conclusion, the burden on the shoulders of Homeland Security is huge especially with the expansion of technological advancements and the misuse of information technology, database systems and information sharing techniques by different terrorist groups to add members from the American community itself by spreading their ideas easily through online networks and attracting curiosity of people. Thus the previously explained techniques and strategies would be a great solution to such problem if well implemented. This doesn't ensure that 100 percent of terror disasters would disappear in the future, but at least, terrorists would think many times before they think of initiating any violent action knowing that there is a lower chance of success than before, and higher risk of failure.

References

Garber, L. (2015). Have We Learned a Lesson? The Boston Marathon Bombings And Information Sharing. Administrative Law Review, 67(1), 221-263.

Kellermann, A. L., & Peleg, K. (2013, May 23). Lessons from Boston. Retrieved November 10, 2017, from http://www.nejm.org.mutex.gmu.edu/doi/citedby/10.1056/NEJMp1305304#t=article#t=cited

Grier, P. (2013, Apr 23). Was boston marathon bombing a US 'intelligence failure'? The Christian Science Monitor Retrieved from https://search-proquest-com.mutex.gmu.edu/docview/1336856858?accountid=14541

Guarino, M. (2013, Jul 04). Fourth of july events: How cities are beefing up security post boston marathon. The Christian Science Monitor Retrieved from https://search-proquest-com.mutex.gmu.edu/docview/1391459755?accountid=14541

Munnell, C., & Todaro, C. (2014). More training, communications funds needed, first responders say. National Defense, 99(729), 16. Retrieved from https://search-proquest-com.mutex.gmu.edu/docview/1553419507?accountid=14541

McCarthy, Andrew C. "If You See Something, Say Nothing." New Criterion, vol. 31, no. 10, June 2013, p. 13. EBSCOhost, mutex.gmu.edu/login?url=http://search.ebscohost.com/login.aspx?direct=true&db=f5h&AN=88134092&site=ehost-live.

MAGNUSON, STEW. "Catching Terrorists Carrying Bombs Still a Tough Problem to Solve." National Defense, vol. 97, no. 715, June 2013, p. 14. EBSCOhost, mutex.gmu.edu/login?url=http://search.ebscohost.com/login.aspx?direct=true&db=mth&AN=91 690028&site=ehost-live.

Pele, K., & Shenhar, I. (2014). Did the U.S. Response to the Marathon Bombings Help or Harm Security? Retrieved October 30, 2017, from https://www.ncbi.nlm.nih.gov/pmc/articles/PMC3926108/#!po=91.6667

Kim, W. (2005). On U.S. homeland security and database technology. Journal of Database Management, 16(1), 1-17. Retrieved from https://search-proquest-com.mutex.gmu.edu/docview/199628603?accountid=14541

Kilburn,John C.,Jr, Costanza, S. E., Metchik, E., & Borgeson, K. (2011). Policing terror threats and false positives: Employing a signal detection model to examine changes in national and local policing strategy between 2001 and 2007. Security Journal, 24(1), 19-36. doi:http://dx.doi.org.mutex.gmu.edu/10.1057/sj.2009.7

Zuckerman, J., Bucci, S. P., & Carafano, J. J. (2013). 60 terrorist plots since 9/11: Continued lessons in domestic counterterrorism. ().The Heritage Foundation. Retrieved from https://search-proquest-com.mutex.gmu.edu/docview/1820753030?accountid=14541

Begley, S. (2001, Sep 24). Will we ever be safe again?; in the wake of the terror attacks, experts in 'homeland defense' are scrambling to protect the nation's public places. A ban on curbside check-in is only the beginning. Newsweek, , 58. Retrieved from https://search-proquest-com.mutex.gmu.edu/docview/214020064?accountid=14541

YOUR KNOWLEDGE HAS VALUE

- We will publish your bachelor's and master's thesis, essays and papers

- Your own eBook and book - sold worldwide in all relevant shops

- Earn money with each sale

Upload your text at www.GRIN.com and publish for free